So THAT'S Where They Came From!

So THAT'S Where They Came From!

By Pat Oliphant

**Andrews McMeel
Publishing**

Kansas City

A MOUNTAIN IN MAINE.

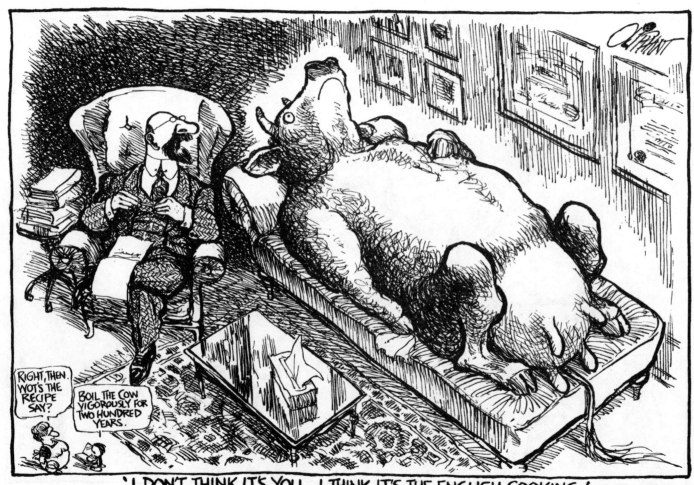

'I DON'T THINK IT'S YOU. I THINK IT'S THE ENGLISH COOKING.'

THE SEASON OPENS IN CALIFORNIA.

AMERICAN JURISPRUDENCE: THE CONTINUING SAGA.

April 11,1996

13

TIANANMEN REVISITED.

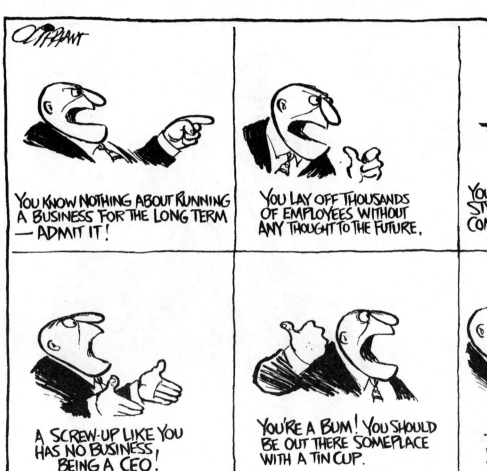

April 19, 1996

SPRING WEDDING.

April 23, 1996

April 29, 1996

May 2, 1996

May 6, 1996

27

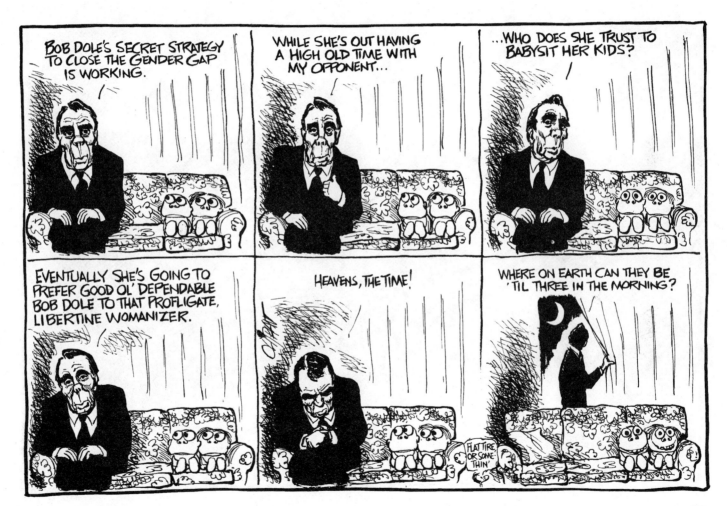

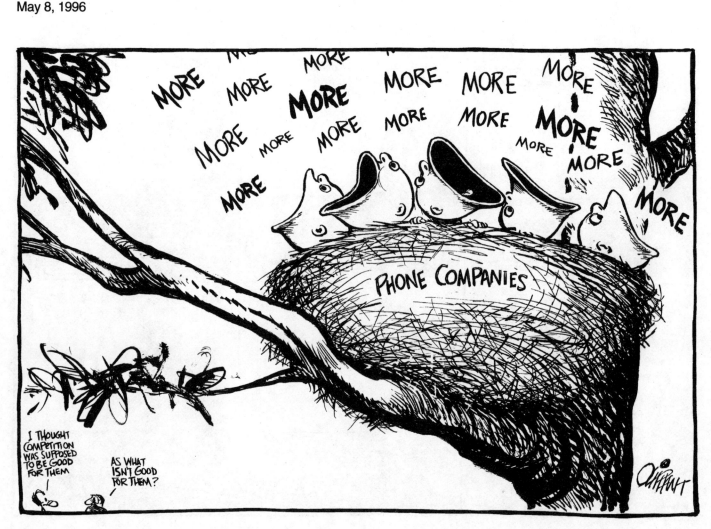

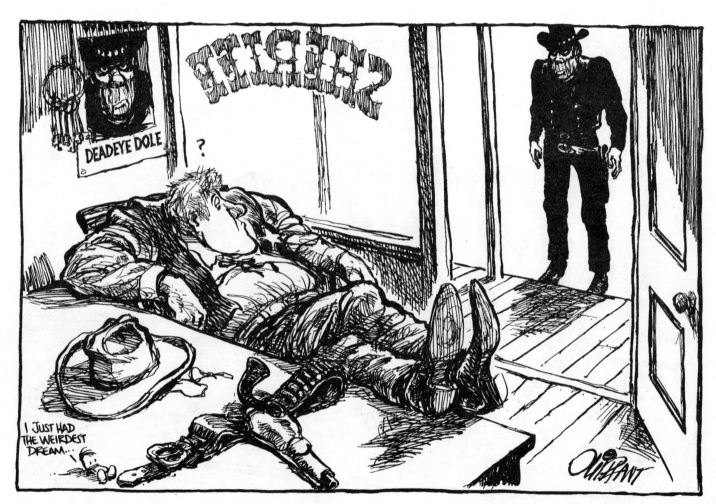

MINIMALISTS.

'NO, I HAVEN'T BEEN DRINKING — THERE ARE COMMUNISTS AT OUR DOOR, BEGGING TO BUY OUR VOTE!'

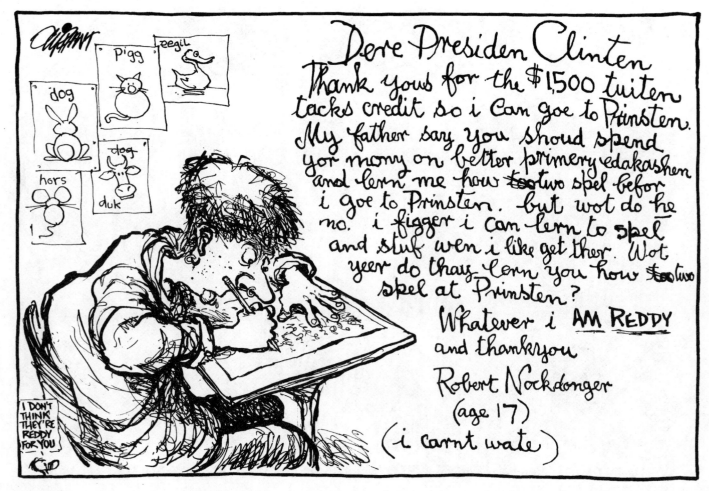

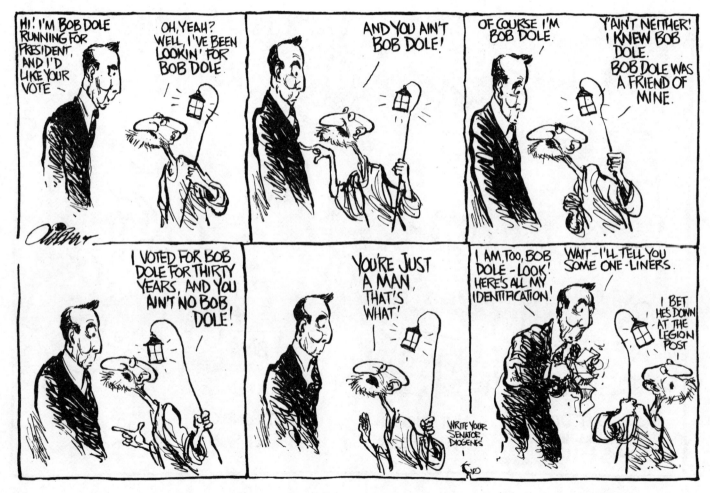

'ONE MORE TIME, MR. YELTSIN!!'

THE AIR SAFETY JUMP TEAM.

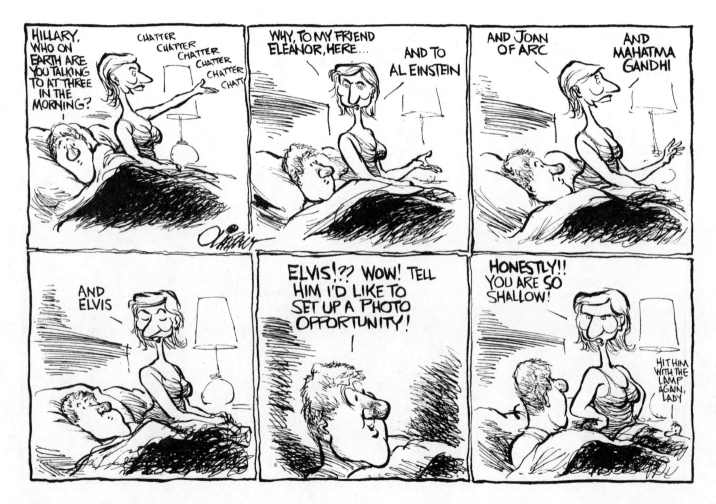

THE GINSBURG BALANCE.

July 10, 1996

56

'HERE'S THE CHOICE, BORIS — GO ON VACATION EARLY, OR LUNCH WITH AL GORE.'

'WE'RE RESCUED, HONEY — THE CRAZED AVENGER IS BACK!'

July 23, 1996

THE CRAZED AVENGER RIDES AGAIN.

SECURITY.

OFFICIAL SWINE *of the* 1996 OLYMPIC GAMES

A WELFARE BILL.

August 5, 1996

'YES, THIS IS THE ADDRESS MR. CLINTON GAVE US.'

SO THAT'S WHERE THEY CAME FROM!

'FROM THE G.O.P. ... HOT DOG, I'VE BEEN INCLUSIONED!'

August 15, 1996

74

BUGS IN THE ROSE GARDEN.

'JUST LISTEN TO THIS GORE CHARACTER! WHY, IF I HAD A SISTER WHO SMOKED AND THEN DIED OF LUNG CANCER, YOU WOULDN'T HEAR ME PUBLICLY WHINING ABOUT IT!'

August 30, 1996

'BILL CLINTON SENT ME.'

September 9, 1996

83

SCENES FROM A MARRIAGE——THE MORRIS HOUSEHOLD.

September 12, 1996

'JUSTIFY MY DAY SADDAM!'

THEIR WELFARE DENIED.

September 19, 1996

90

October 7, 1996

99

JUST DON'T OPEN THE DOOR.

October 17, 1996

A KANSAS CHILDHOOD.

October 23, 1996

109

'I COULD VOTE FOR YOU, AND YOU COULD VOTE FOR ME...'

THE SEARCH RESUMES.

November 4, 1996

'THE 3,367TH JOHN HUANG IS NOW VOTING...'

115

November 5, 1996

FOUR MORE YEARS OF WHOMEVER.

November 11, 1996

121

November 12, 1996

THE ALL-NEW GINGRICH PUDDING... PROOF OF WHICH COMES LATER.

WHY WE SEND THEM ON TRIPS.

'HAND ME UP ONE O' THEM JANET RENO DOLLS.'

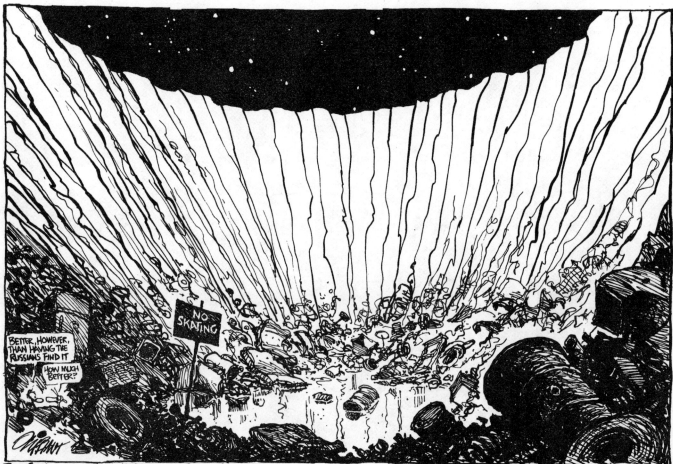

THE GOOD NEWS IS, WATER HAS BEEN FOUND ON THE MOON. THE BAD NEWS IS, WATER HAS BEEN FOUND ON THE MOON.

December 5, 1996

133

December 9, 1996

December 10, 1996

December 16, 1996

December 18, 1996

December 19, 1996

'...IN SMALL BILLS, NO CHECKS.'

THE PROPRIETOR.

January 15, 1997

149

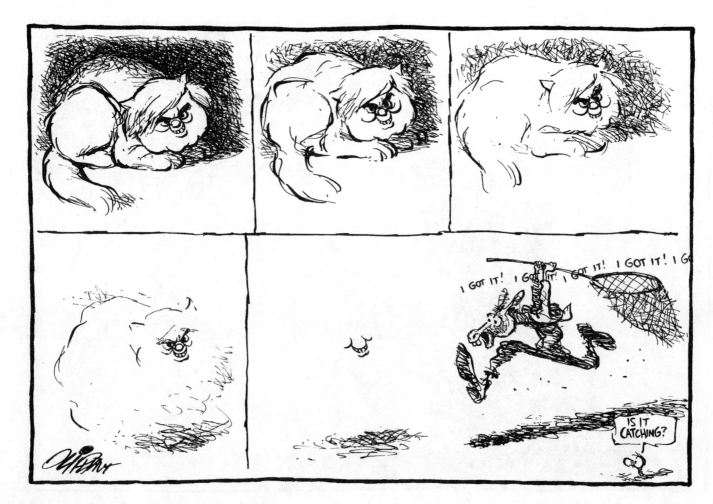

'I'M SORRY WE CAN'T HELP YOU, MS. JONES... WE'RE DEMOCRATS.'

AN ITALIAN SHOE-MAKER IS PRESENTED WITH AN ADVERTISING CONCEPT.

AT A D.N.C. COFFEE.

January 30, 1997

'NOBODY UNDERSTANDS A CIVILIZER.'